*To my little pirates, G. & P.*

# Lucilinburhuc's Treasure

Marie-Isabelle Callier

Once upon a time, a magnificent ship ran aground right in the middle of a city park. Surrounded by trees, swings, canal locks, and water pumps, the ship had become a favorite spot for small pirates and sailors.

That morning, two brothers had taken over the command of the vessel. Red Beard was at the top of the look-out post while Black Beard took over the helm. Their names and posts thus determined, a brand-new odyssey could begin.

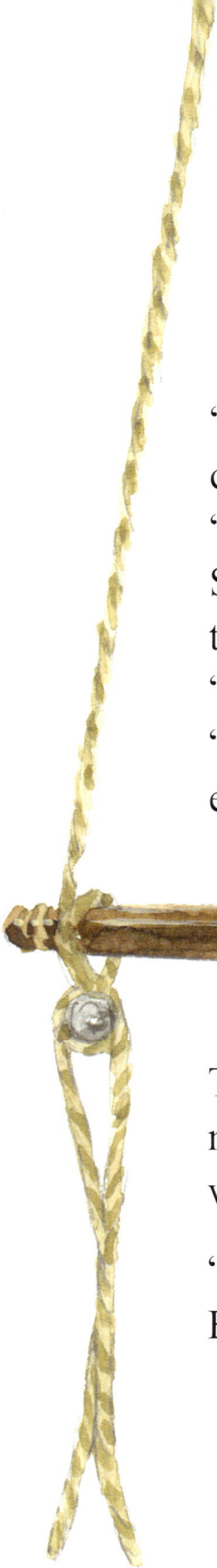

“Cast off! All sails set!”
cried Black Beard.
“Batten down the hatches!
Secure the latches!”
thundered Red Beard.
“To the starboard side!”
“No! Port side, bleary-
eyed!”

They were already
navigating on the high seas
when Red Beard called out.

“Bottle at sea!
Bottle at sea!”

Fishing the bottle from the ocean, they pulled out an old, well-worn parchment and began to decipher.

They say in times of old
A pact in the city was signed.
With a thousand pieces of gold,
The new lord's coffers were lined.
But his castle built,
The city founded,
He learned that his lady love,
Had hidden the treasure trove.
Everywhere in the ancient city
Small pieces of parchment will be littered.
To encounter the first clue
Just let the music guide you...

"Music? What music?" began Black Beard.
"Look!" said Red Beard, turning over the parchment. "A map!"

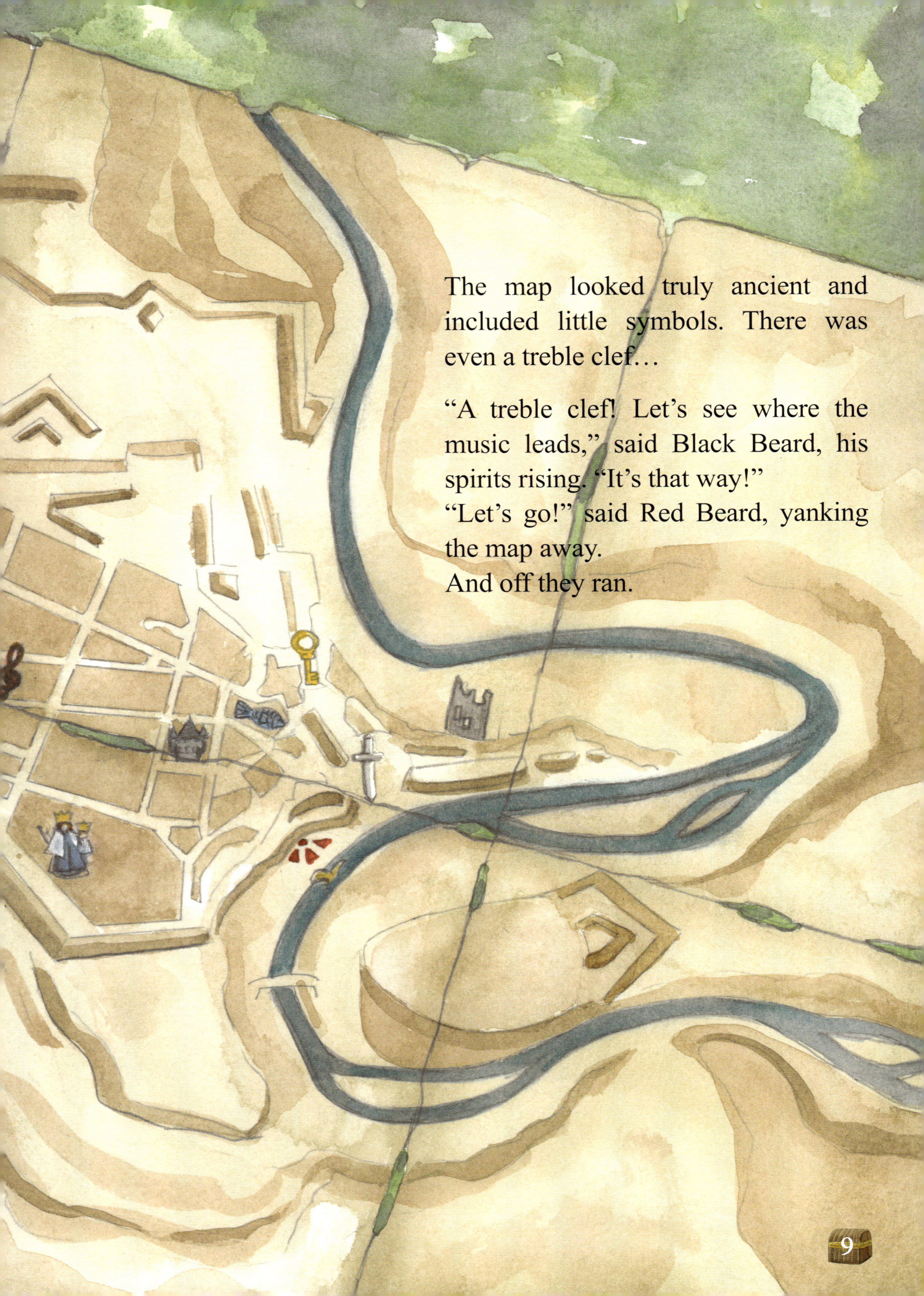

The map looked truly ancient and included little symbols. There was even a treble clef…

“A treble clef! Let’s see where the music leads,” said Black Beard, his spirits rising. “It’s that way!”
“Let’s go!” said Red Beard, yanking the map away.
And off they ran.

They came to the *Place d'Armes* and hurried towards the bandstand where they found the first parchment.

A famous lady holds the second one
High atop her Bastion.
No Grand Duchess,
Though dressed in a gold gown,
Not a Princess either,
Yet she wears a crown.
Who is she?

"Dressed in a gold gown, a crown… it's the *Gëlle Fra*, the Golden Lady!" exclaimed Red Beard.
"I'm sure you're right… but let me see that map," said Black Beard.
"Hold on, let me check. Yes! She's on the map, too!" said Red Beard.
"You're always holding the map! I want to see it, too! Show it to me!" demanded Black Beard. And with no warning, he pulled on the map… and tore it apart.
"Now look what you've done!" cried Red Beard.
"Well, if you had shared…" retorted Black Beard, defending himself.
"Well, aren't you the clever one!" replied Red Beard. "If that's the way you want things to be, why don't you just go your way, and I'll go mine!"
"And why not? Maybe I'll find the treasure before you do!"
"So you want this to be a race? Well, that's alright by me! Death to the treasure!" said Red Beard as he took off running.
*Ah! So that's the way it is!* thought Black Beard. *He who laughs last, laughs best! I'll be the one to find it.*

And as quick as lightning, he ran off in the opposite direction.

At Beck's Bastion, Red Beard found the next parchment at the feet of the *Gëlle Fra*. The riddle was hidden behind the warrior's helmet.

Another Lady will help you.
Celestial is her crown.
The Queen of Heaven consoles
All those who are cast down.
In her house here on earth
To your wishes she will give birth.

The Queen of Heaven… who was Queen of Heaven?
On his map, there was a lady and a baby, and both were wearing a crown…
Perhaps the Virgin Mary and the Baby Jesus?
Yes, that's it! The Queen of Heaven was Our Lady… *Notre Dame!*
He took off immediately towards the cathedral.

The bells began to ring, just as they would on high feast days.

At the same time, Black Beard had headed towards the Palace of the Grand Duke. If there were a treasure to be found, surely it would be hidden in a castle. One castle was certainly worth another, so he had nothing to lose by trying. The only problem was that he couldn't get in. He began to look for another clue in the surrounding area but found nothing on the facade or in the sentry gatehouse.

Finally, he found a clue stuck between the iron railings of the Red Lion.

What did you think, young impatient one?
The castle you seek has seen a thousand years' suns.
Go back further, way before
And find the oldest marketplace of yore
Another message waits there in store.

There was an open-air market on the *Place Guillaume* and another one at *Glacis* Field… but the oldest marketplace of yore was, without a doubt, Old Market Square, also called Fish Market Square. Hey! There was even a little fish on his map!
At last, he was onto something… a solid clue!

Mir wölle bleiwe
wat mir sin

Because Black Beard was looking for something very old, he was surprised when he came to Fish Market Square and saw how modern it looked. He began to explore the little narrow streets that led out from the square, thinking he might find clues from long ago.

Underneath the Luxembourg motto, *Mir wöllen bleiwe war mir sin* (We want to remain what we are), he discovered a small piece of parchment.

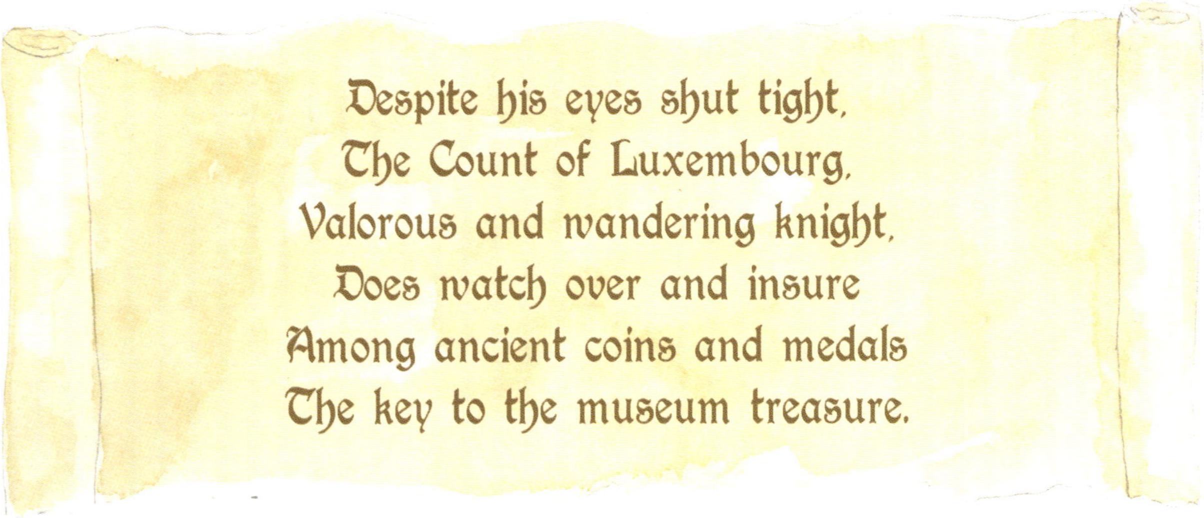


"A museum? According to my map, it's close by..."

He retraced his steps and found himself in front of a contemporary white structure on Fish Market Square. The building was none other than the National Museum of History and Art. He entered and began to visit the various rooms.

At the same time, Red Beard was going from one mystery to the next. He found a clue at *Notre Dame*.

From Europe's most beautiful balconies
Listen to Alzette's fantasies
Perhaps you will hear the melodic wish
Of the beautiful half-woman, half-fish.

"The most beautiful balconies… that must be the *Chemin de la Corniche*, the path along the cliff. And the beautiful half-woman half-fish is Melusina!" said Red Beard, suddenly overcome with worry.

Melusina was a figure surrounded by legend and mystery. Some said she was a fairy, others a witch! But above all, she was the wife of Siegfried, the first Count of Luxembourg, the founder of the city.

**The new lord... the city founded...** those were the words of the first parchment! Red Beard was finally sure that he, too, was on the right track. He might even get there first.

Again, he departed. On the *Chemin de la Corniche*, he unearthed the fourth parchment.

When he opened it, a strange voice murmured.

> Upon this rock, Lucilinburhuc
> Was built long ago.
> Since then, passages have been hewn
> Inside, far below.
> Advance towards the entranceway,
> The castle bridge cross over.
> Close to the stairway
> One last clue you will discover.

The voice sent shivers down his spine! He wasn't feeling too sure of himself. Besides, he could no longer count on this map which had come to an end… Black Beard had the other half.

*If only they had not fought!* he thought with regret.

But Red Beard stayed calm and started to think. Lucilinburhuc, otherwise known as "little castle," was the first castle built long, long ago on Bock's massive rock. And the passages were casemates, or small rooms built in the thickness of the castle walls.

But he was no longer in such a hurry at the idea of going there all by himself. He decided to wait for Black Beard at the entrance… perhaps he was already there.

In fact, Black Beard was not far away. Under the bust of John the Blind, he found a precious key with a message.

In the church of the archangel
The one who fought the demon
Atop the stained-glass window
The bishop gives a blessing.
Indeed, this holy place
Was built after a wedding.
Find these noble lords' names
And you will find their dwelling.

A stained-glass window, a church… an archangel…
The archangel who had fought hard against the devil was Saint Michael for whom the city's first church was named. That was easy. Plus, a sword confirmed the spot on the map. Without hesitating, Black Beard left the museum and headed toward Saint Michael's Church.

Close to the entrance, the Archangel – the vanquished Devil at his feet – welcomed Black Beard. He entered the church and began to examine the stained-glass windows, one by one.

A date caught his eye: "987."
An inscription, too: "Consecration by Egbert."

And a couple: a noble lord and lady, next to an archbishop.
This was the stained-glass window! It portrayed Archbishop Egbert blessing the first small castle chapel, still in the same place, years after the founding of the city in 963. And the noble lord was surely Siegfried, the first Count of Luxembourg, and the lady, his wife, Melusina.

The only thing left for him to find was the spot where the castle stood. Surely a parchment would help him with that. He began to look.

He found it in the lectern's beak!

Atop its unattainable rock
Our proud castle was, at one epoch,
Truly beautiful, ravishing.
Today, alas, our little keep
Is no longer quite so appealing.
For centuries now, I, Melusina
Return ofttimes to this arena,
Hiding in the well of its underground cells.

"Underground chambers in a rock. I was sure about those casemates," said Black Beard who took off even faster towards the Bock.

Was he ever happy to find his brother there! Their quarrel forgotten, the two brothers shared their discoveries: Black Beard, his precious key, and Red Beard, the map of the casemates he had found next to the stairway. One last message was written on the back side.

They headed directly down to the passages which were becoming more and more gloomy. Black Beard pulled the little key out of his pocket. It began to shine, and illuminated their map in the darkness.

"Look at this spot! It's brighter!" said Red Beard.
"That must be the well," answered Black Beard. "Let's go!"

And that's how they arrived at Melusina's well and their reward. Using the little key, they opened the trunk and found dozens and dozens of shiny coins in the bottom! Gold coins? They decided to bite, just to be sure. The coins were made of chocolate! Lucky for them, for they were starting to get hungry.
Surely, it was time for a snack.
It was time to go home.

Eager to show off their loot and brag about their adventures, they headed back, happy as could be.

The very next day, they would set off in search of a new scheme. And once again, they would triumph!
*Together*, they were an unbeatable team.

The End

108, rue de l'Alzette
L-4010 Esch-sur-Alzette
Luxembourg

editions@schortgen.lu
www.editions-schortgen.lu

Illustrations and text: Marie-Isabelle Callier
English Translation: Jane Singleton Paul

Layout: Schortgen*grafic*
Printing: Schortgen*bookprint*

ISBN: 978-99959-36-46-4